BUZZ TAKES OVER

Carmel Reilly
Karen Young

Rigby

www.Rigby.com
1-800-531-5015

Rigby Focus Forward

This Edition © 2009 Rigby, a Harcourt Education Imprint

Published in 2007 by Nelson Australia Pty Ltd ACN: 058 280 149
A Cengage Learning company

1 2 3 4 5 6 7 8 374 14 13 12 11 10 09 08 07
Printed and bound in China

Buzz Takes Over
ISBN-13   978-1-4190-3743-6
ISBN-10   1-4190-3743-9

BUZZ TAKES OVER

Carmel Reilly

Karen Young

Contents

Chapter 1

HEADING HOME

Buzz and Zip were heading home
to planet Zero.

"I've done all the driving on this trip,"
Zip said to Buzz.
"It's your turn now."

"My turn!" yelled Buzz.
"I'm a terrible driver!"

"Look," said Zip.
"Just set the autopilot,
and we'll be back in no time."

Before Buzz could say anything,
Zip climbed into one of the
sleeping pods and closed the door.

"He's right.
It can't be too hard," said Buzz,
pushing the autopilot button.

But as he sat down,
the computer suddenly lit up.
"Warning! Black hole!" it said.

6

"A black hole!"
Buzz waved his arms around.
"What am I going to do?"
he screamed.

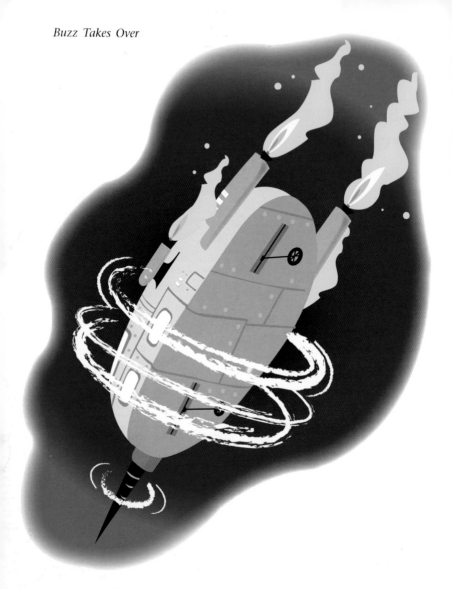

The ship zoomed forward
and started to roll.
So did Buzz ...

"Oh," said Buzz as he grabbed
on to the controls.
"Ah!" he said as he flew
against the window.
"Ow!" he said as he crashed
onto the floor.

Chapter 2

THE BLUE GALAXY

As suddenly as it started,
the rolling stopped.
Buzz picked himself up off the floor
and looked out the window.
"Goodness me!" he said.

PRESS

WARNING!
BLACK
HOLE!

AUTO
PILOT

The black hole had taken him
into another galaxy—a blue galaxy.

Buzz began to think.
"Blue galaxy ..." he said.
"What do I know about
a blue galaxy?"

PRESS

SPACE
PIRATES
AHEAD!

AUTO
PILOT

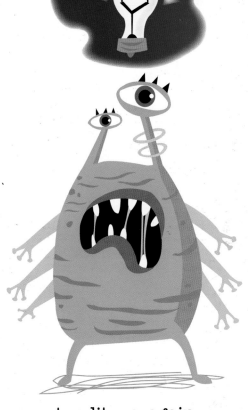

The computer lit up again.
"Space pirates ahead!" it warned.

"Of course, that's it!" shouted Buzz.
"The blue galaxy is home
to space pirates."

Chapter 3

PIRATES AHEAD

Buzz took a deep breath
and looked at the controls.
He had to get out of here—and fast.
He saw a big red button
and pushed it.
He closed his eyes
and crossed all his arms and fingers
as the ship zoomed forward.

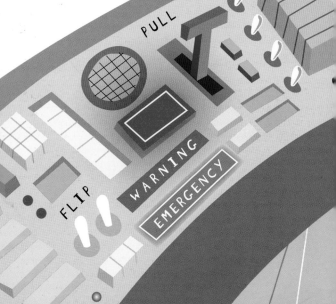

PULL

WARNING

EMERGENCY

FLIP

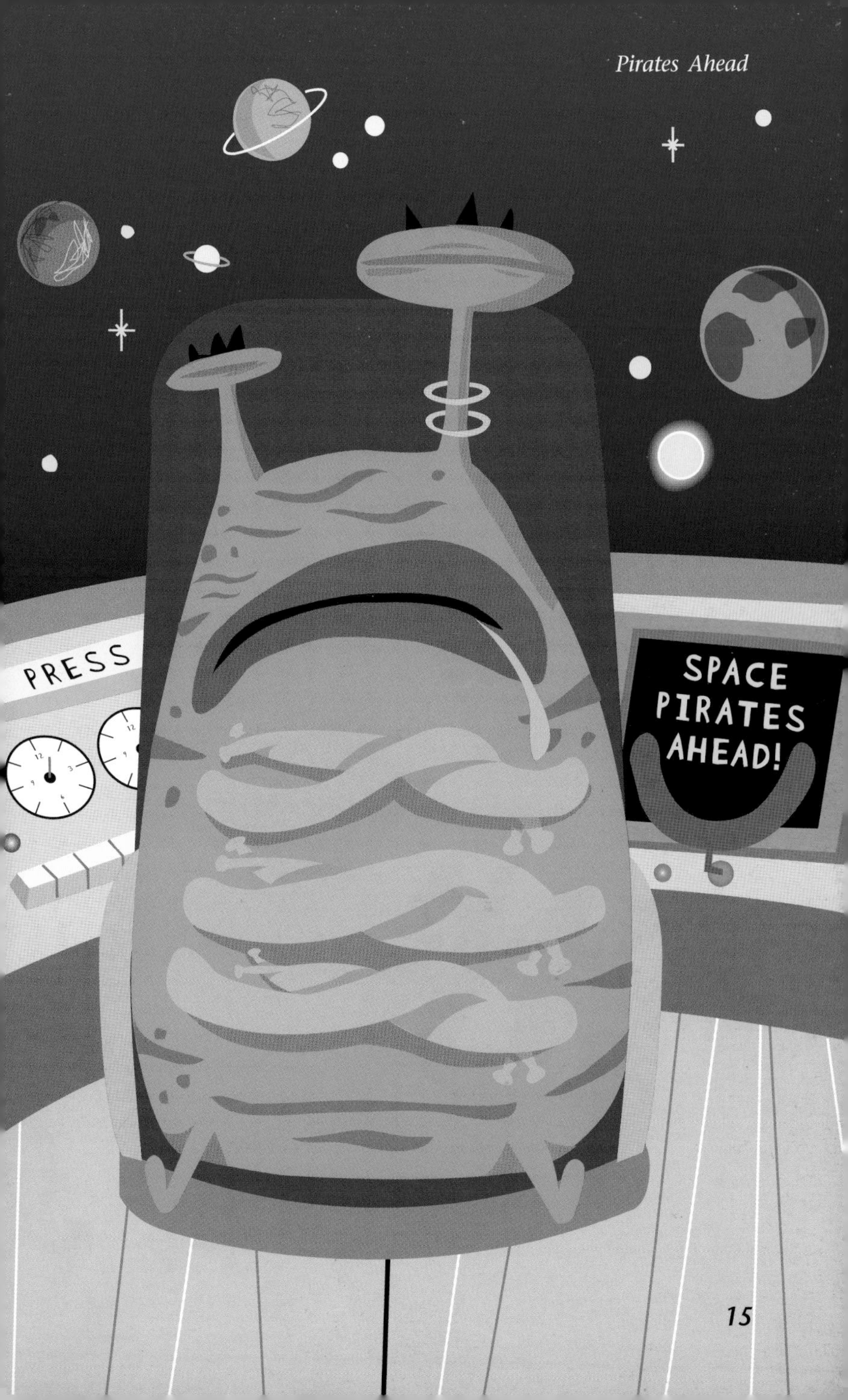
PRESS
SPACE PIRATES AHEAD!

Buzz opened his eyes
and looked outside.
He screamed.
He hadn't zoomed away
from the pirates
—he'd zoomed right up to them.

16

Soon he was so close he could see
the whites of their eyes!

Then Buzz did what he always did
when something went wrong.
He screamed, ran around,
and waved his arms in the air.
But as soon as he ran, he tripped.

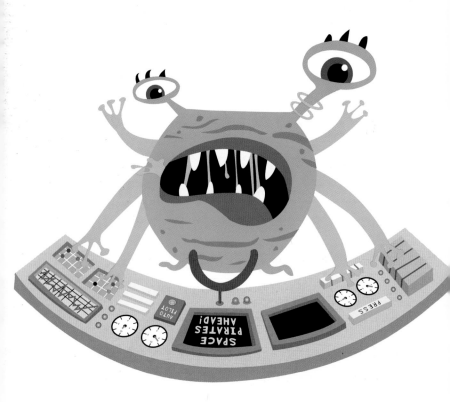

Buzz didn't know how many buttons
he pushed when he crashed
onto the controls.
But one of them must have worked.
The ship zoomed over
the pirates' ship
and went deep into space.

Chapter 4

ANOTHER BLACK HOLE

The ship landed in
a very dark part of the galaxy.
The computer lit up again.
"Black hole! Black hole!" it said.

"Oh, no! Not again!" said Buzz,
grabbing onto the controls
as the ship zoomed forward
and started to roll.

After what seemed like
a very long time,
the ship stopped rolling.
Buzz got up and went to the window.

"Goodness me!" he said,
shaking his head.
"How did that happen?
We're almost home!"

As the ship landed, Zip woke up.
"Did anything exciting happen?"
he asked.
Buzz opened his mouth
to say something ...
but he knew
Zip was never going to believe him
in a million years!